WATCHING OURSELVES

Poems

by

Mark Belair

Published by Unsolicited Press
www.unsolicitedpress.com
Copyright © 2017 Mark Belair
All Rights Reserved.
Unsolicited Press Books are distributed to the trade by
Ingram.
ISBN: 978-0-9980872-7-6
Cover Design: Barbara Amstutz

ACKNOWLEDGMENTS

Grateful acknowledgement is made to the editors of the following journals, who first published these poems:

Alabama Literary Review: "Fashion Statement," "The Summer Night," "Skeeter"
Atlanta Review: "one thanksgiving"
the Briar Cliff Review: "Leavings"
the Broken Plate: "After the Rain"
the Cincinnati Review: "Listeners"
Cold Mountain Review: "The Caricature"
Crack the Spine Literary Magazine: "perky"
Forge: "The Image," "Quiet," "Snow Man," "Fresh Fruit," "Small Town," "Looking Elsewhere," "A Moment in the Sum," "After the Museum," "Bedtime," "Winter Sky"
Ginosko Literary Journal: "geography"
Green Hills Literary Lantern: "The Farmhouse," "The Watch"
the Griffin: "Aunt Alice"
Iodine Poetry Journal: "Snowflakes"
Poet Lore: "collecting"
Poetry East: "Bread"
Riprap Journal: "Shadow Casting"
Stand Magazine: "The Heating Pipe"
the Summerset Review: "Billie"
the Tower Journal: "new britain"
Tiger's Eye: A Journal of Poetry: "Drumming Essentials"

Table of Contents

watching ourselves
COME FROM THE PAST

The Farmhouse

My great-grandfather's farmhouse in Maine,
where my father spent his early boyhood, is

now a gift shop. You can walk in—we did—
and cruise the unchanged layout of rooms.

This one, my dad said, bore his grandmother's
cast-iron stove, one so high off the floor he'd

wriggle under it during the deep winter cold,
a practice he shared with the snuggling cat.

Out back stood the woods my father explored.
But long gone are the chicken coops—chickens,

for a while, a decent bonus business for them.
The updated house—all re-shingled, re-roofed,

and re-plastered—now smells of scented candles
and squeaks with the spin of the postcard rack.

But the hidden timbers are original, timbers so
stout and fitted they make further renovation

impossible; timbers fashioned from trees that
grew in and were formed by this humble plot

on which they still work—this homestead
of my father, of myself.

one thanksgiving

in the mid-1950s / my grandfather won a turkey raffle at
the mill in maine where he pulled shifts as an electrician

he bragged of his luck to his wife and two grown
daughters then / on the appointed day / strode up to
the mill's loading dock where he was handed a good-
sized turkey that was / to his surprise / alive

he tucked it tight under his arm / walked home with a
frown / then stuck it in the basement / until he'd kill it
for thanksgiving dinner

as that day approached / my grandmother / having
dutifully cared for the bird / told my grandfather it was
time to behead the thing / so she could pluck and clean
and stuff it

my grandfather descended the basement stairs / with his
newly sharpened ax / but minutes later he trudged back
up / and said to my grandmother / *i can't do it / not today
anyway / he looked me in the eyes*

the same thing happened the next day / and the day
after that / my grandfather climbing back upstairs / his
long ax clean / to report that / once again / the bird had
looked him in the eyes

his daughters / of course / found this development /
deliciously humorous

but after a week of it / my grandmother / old farm girl
that she was / before a fire destroyed her family's
homestead / displacing them from quebec / stomped
down and wrung the turkey's neck / without giving it a
thought

but my grandfather wouldn't eat that turkey /
thanksgiving or not / nor would he taste the sandwiches
that followed / or the turkey vegetable soup

nor would my frowning grandfather meet / night after
night at the dinner table / long after the turkey was
gone / my grandmother's eyes

The Heating Pipe

A silver heating pipe
ran up from my grandparent's flat to ours
in the old clapboard house in Maine,
and I'd sit by it, cross-legged,
late afternoons, waiting for a sign.

For when my grandfather came home
from his shift at the mill, he'd shower, then—
with an old red, adjustable wrench—
bang three times on the pipe

and my three-year-old legs would
thump downstairs to play
monster-man with him
and ride across the kitchen floor
on a throw rug he'd pull

and eat forbidden chocolates
with him behind closed doors
until he'd tire and take his nap,
me sleeping, too, across

his high barrel chest,
big baby head
rising and falling
with his every breath.

Then one night
he went to the movies
and, suffering a heart attack,
never came back.

But still I sat
by the heating pipe late afternoons,
absorbing my loss
like heat from the pipe,

baking into myself
a layer
of melancholy
loyal to my grandfather.

The Watch

Someone
kept to a corner
of a dream, watching it
with me, until I glanced up
to see my grandfather
not in the memories
my three-year-old mind
enshrined after he died
but from my present perspective—
aged into the decade of his death—
noting the features we share
and those we don't
until I wept with joy
at this wondrous reunion—
though his gentle smile
told me that our reunion
was all one-sided, told me
that his love, lavished
upon my toddler self,
had not been lost
but had been, after all,
at the edge of every dream,
sleeping or waking,
keeping watch.

watching ourselves
WATCH OTHERS

The Image

The still image
of a maintenance man
in uniform, his name
stitched into his shirt, holds
on the flat screen TV
of an art installation—one
set to snap random shots—
that faces out a museum window
while the worker, unaware,
orders coffee from a street vendor
and talks about his job
and its morning annoyances, the screen
behind him keeping him
as he was
as he gets his coffee
and moves on into his day, his held
past seeming to watch him
walk away, to watch itself
being forgotten.

After the Rain

passes, two young mothers
deep in conversation

let their two little girls run out from
under a striped café awning and play

in a world made newly present
by the sudden absence of rain;

a world really no different
from the one before the downpour

but for a skim-coat of wetness
the shower painted on everything.

Yet the girls prance and play
beneath the briskly clearing sky

as if in a tizzy, giggly romance
with this fresh, rainless world

while their mothers, still under cover, talk on
about husbands, parents, and money—each

checking, now and then, on the girls
and the ever changing sky.

Quiet

A silver-soft day, quiet
as rustled bullets,

as bitter thoughts too long
held, as a man on his back

contemplating the clouds
while calmly calculating

who is
to blame.

Snow Man

An old man combs his thin, white hair with a white plastic fork.

He wears a white sweatshirt and white sweatpants.

Two overstuffed, white plastic bags sit on the park bench next to him.

Then he leans forward, folds his hands, hangs his head, and weeps.

I stand beneath my black umbrella and watch.

It's raining out.

13

Listeners

All the listeners
are out tonight at the sidewalk cafés, casual
clusters of them at scattered tables,
huddled in, each assembly alert
to someone speaking
so quietly all I hear
is the silence of the listening,
listening so intense
as to seem to create
circles of attention
that, rising and gathering,
form the great, resonant, sheltering
silence of the night.

watching ourselves
TRY TO BECOME

new britain

black pipes running lengthwise / seemed made for me
to climb / until my arm got pulled so hard/   i felt my
shoulder pop out

mr gibson's dachshund / poops there / my mother furtively
hissed / about a scratchy patch of grass / beyond the
black-pipe walkway fence

then she glanced up warily / to the old stooped cuss
himself / standing watch at his front window/ dark with
suspicion of little children

mr gibson was our landlord / one who made his only
tenant / pay weekly / in person / in cold / as my father
mysteriously put it / cash

mr gibson didn't attend to the nasty dachshund
himself / one of his two / grown / grim / unmarried /
daughters did that

*

next door to us lived six-year-old twins / wayne and
wesley / who / that year / flushed a sack of small red
potatoes down their toilet

thinking / like the twins / that flushing toilets made
magic / i couldn't grasp why all the grown-ups made
such a stern / disapproving fuss

*

in the hushed / gleaming store / where my father sold

16

jewelry / i'd stand at stiff attention beneath my cowboy
hat or sailor's cap / while perfume-stinky salesladies

gushed at me and my big sister / their pearl necklaces /
and heavy bosoms / dangling / in our squirmy faces

*

on weekdays / my sister went to school / only four / i
did not / i stayed home and played in the freedom of the
wide linoleum floors

*

some saturdays my father / snapping scissors / and i /
cheering him on / chased my sister around our four
rooms / threatening to snip her long / obnoxious braids
off

we'd trap her / she'd scream / and the tense / thrilling
moment would come / when i'd half hope this would be
the day / my father would actually do it / *teach a lesson to*

the stuck-up brat / and half hope he wouldn't / a dad who
mauls his children / even a snobby big sister / no one
wants

*

sundays in the park / i'd run downhill / my mother
sitting on a picnic blanket / me timing my loss of
control to when my tumble would safely land me / in
her warm / pillowy / lap

*

then my father got promoted and we moved from new
britain to another store in the connecticut chain / me
hauling these disconnected memories / that i finger now
like oddly mixed heirlooms in an old jewelry box /

17

jewels that can't be strung together on any strand i
know / so jewels of memory / i know / i can trust

geography

my childhood home / an old / clapboard / two-family
affair in a connecticut mill town /sat on a side street that
inclined up to main / an incline that made me who i am
today

across the tilted street from us / an obese florist lived
above the small / fussy shop from which she banned
children / having none herself / and from which she
sent her older / cancer-stricken husband out on
deliveries / claiming / with a theatrical sigh i heard from
outside / that the hill was just too much

next door to us stood a fine baptist church / the black
worshippers / dressed to the nines / flooding downhill
sunday mornings to praise god with joyful hymns and
tambourines / all too festive for us grim / silent
catholics whose cold / bleak church was reached / more
appropriately/ it seemed to us / by climbing up

an auto body shop clanked on our other flank / young
mechanics with ducktails and greasy hands repairing
battered cars right in the road itself / one getting his leg
crushed when a raised car / spitting its jack / went for a
downhill roll

and a set of lost brakes on a local dairy truck / cost my
best friend freddy / knocked off his new red bike / his
life

19

but the incline to main was not the only fact of
geography to form me / not at all / for there are four
seasons in connecticut / dense woods / lush lakes / and
outcroppings of rock that remember / through long
wintry nights / the warmth of the sun

perky

one night / our parents went ballroom dancing / so my
sister and i / to amuse ourselves / thought we'd free
perky / our old blue parakeet

we closed all the windows / so perky couldn't actually
escape / then opened his cage to let him / for the first
time we could recall / fly about a bit

perky stepped right up to the lip of his door / leaped out
then / to our open horror / and stifled hilarity / failed
adequately to fly

perky smacked on a table / shot into a wall / soared up
to a ceiling corner then / chirping crazily / crashed to
the floor

we finally finagled poor perky / back into his cage /
with the help of our father's old crusty fishing net

and when our parents returned from their rare night
out / flushed / tipsy / talkative / bumbling into tables /
we stared at them / unsure whether to laugh or cry

collecting

the farmhouse never had a doorbell / so i rapped / as
usual / on the pane of glass in the door / to get the
money for having made a week of morning newspaper
deliveries / and

the farmer / old / intense / bald / rarely seen by me /
parted the curtain in the door window / and stared at
me / a long time / with one blue eye / then

let the curtain drop / and his footsteps faded away /
while i stood in the cold / not knowing what to do /
perhaps he'd gone to get the money / or was refusing
me the money / perhaps that deadpan look was a joke /
or he was senile / or just plain nuts / then

i heard his wife's familiar / though now lowly scolding /
voice / while her footsteps scurried toward the door /
which she opened with relief at finding me still there / if
in bewilderment / then with a forced smile / she gave
me the sixty-five cents / after which

she politely squeezed the door shut / and i / rooted to
the spot by my bafflement / noticed that the door
window curtain was slightly parted / so i tiptoed up and
peeked inside

to see / down the dim hall / her exasperation with

him / expressed by the wag of her finger / the tilt of her
torso / her blind gestures toward the door / and the
tone of her muffled words / while he

listened with a sly grin / one not crazed but pleased / it
appeared / at having yet again upended all expectations
of conventional behavior / a game you could see he
more delighted in the more it unhinged her / until

she seemed / after having said her piece / to sigh with
stoic acceptance / to sigh with a love that finds it
infuriating to love the beloved / but does / a
development that made me withdraw as if caught in my
spying / or from having seen something alarming /
which

at fourteen / i had / for with that sigh both the farmer
and his wife seemed to regain a stunning youthfulness in
their bodies and faces / as if the farmer's mischief / and
his wife's vexation / then forbearing forgiveness /
ratified a ritual of loyalty

to roles they long ago had assumed on mutual
assignment / roles that transported them back to their
courting days / roles conceived within moments /
perhaps / of their confessed infatuations / in that

dangerous / fateful vacuum / that i / a sober soul with a
secret crush / on a mischievous girl who rode my bus /
felt suddenly whirling into

watching ourselves
TRY LOVE

Fresh Fruit

The fruit stand sprouted
two colorful umbrellas
beneath which
the gentle Caribbean fruit man
handed an apple or a plum or a peach—
I was too far away to tell which—
to a girl—how young was she?—
in her tight, white top
old enough to sport a figure—
and the girl set the fruit
to her nose and inhaled its sweet fragrance
and the fruit man and the young girl
laughed, it was what she wanted
so, with a precocious toss of her long brown hair,
she took it,
it was hers.

Small Town

A young town cop
and a high school cheerleader

met
and fell in love.

After years of increasingly
complicated marriage,

they found
an old home movie

of the cheerleader
twirling in a Memorial Day parade.

And as she marched through
the town's one crossroad,

the cop stood
holding traffic back.

Neither
knew each other at the time.

Neither
now remembers that parade.

But each remembers
how heartbreakingly

happy
they were.

Fashion Statement

After trilling good bye
in her best party voice while
waving back, she confidently model-steps
down from what seems
a glamorous restaurant gathering,

strides with strict savoir-faire
around the reflective-glass corner, immediately
stops, evicts whatever kept her hair stacked high
and shakes it all out, tucks her black, gauzy, bejeweled
scarf into her stylish purse from which she pulls

two flip-flops
she drops to the sidewalk
then—laying a hand on her companion's shoulder—
she bends one leg up behind her and,
off-balance, blindly

tugs a wicked high heel
off, stubs her foot into a flip-flop, then
repeats the awkward maneuver for the other foot
and stuffs both shoes into the purse, her
companion, all this time,

jabbering on
about some guy at work—
was it a company party?—trying to muscle him
out, but she can't seem to focus on him, her
face revealing no goal

29

but one: to return—her fashion
performance done—to her preferred state of
fashion disaster, which is fortunate for him,
for as she flip-flops away she casually takes his
arm and, restored, tilts her head to listen.

Skeeter

Considering the open red convertible
and its dreadlocked driver approaching

the stoplight at my crosswalk, I expected
bouncing reggae or kick-drum-driven rap

to rule the soft summer night, so was
surprised to hear the helpless, plaintive cry

of Skeeter Davis lamenting lost love—
a loss, for her, "the end of the world"—

the driver—sporting sunglasses in the dark—
belting along, shoulders twisting with grief,

and I found myself, while crossing the street,
chiming in, as transported by utter devastation

as they, all our accents
clashing, the convertible,

at the change of the light, tearing off
into the night, their voices fading, me

left humming of what
bonds us all.

watching ourselves
REFLECT

Cars

Tires hiss by
on the wet street outside
as I regard my grandfather
in a dark picture frame, his
life brief as the sweep
of this unseen car, a car
receding as unremarkably
as the friend's car
he should have stayed in
that rainy 4th of July night
of 1929
when he was 24.

Instead, he switched, in
the holiday party commotion,
to the one with the quietly
drunk stranger driving, the grisly
accident site, found hours later,
still and silent
as this photograph, my grandfather's
searching face, turning toward
us, held
motion-blurred.

Leavings

Beneath a winter-bared tree:
pigeon droppings

dense on the sidewalk
as a drip canvas by Jackson Pollack.

And knotted pairs of sneakers dangling
from the arm to an East Village stoplight.

And in an old, bloated box in my closet,
a red cowboy shirt

with mother-of-pearl buttons
from when I was four;

and beneath it
a crumpled kindergarten

report card
from when I was five;

and under that the dark,
dented drumsticks

of my grandfather
whose early death

in a car wreck—
when I learned

of the ancient
tragedy at six—

tore my heart out
and left it

where it still beats:
at arm's length.

watching ourselves
CROSS OVER

"It is not upon you alone the dark patches fall…"

Walt Whitman
"Crossing Brooklyn Ferry"

Crossing Over
The Perfect Host

You suffer without reason.
Without due cause.

But suffering
is what it is.

What trauma started this?
What hidden flaw?

You felt okay,
seemed like others

then, one day—
did not.

Or were you infected,
when young,

with some grim parasite
(unacknowledged loss?

subtle cause for doubt?)
that found,

in your soft, budding soul,
the perfect host?

Jargon

The Pulse
meant the general, blind drive to live.

The Pushes,
more particular impulses.

The Nocturnal
named the wish to regress to the womb.

The Patches,
sudden, fragmentary memories.

The Naught
stood for all negative, destructive urges.

The Axle Hole
described the core of nothingness

The Wheel
of your personality spun around.

Sunken People
defined those

Boxed In
like you, but who no longer resisted the

Clinging Vines
of their troubled pasts.

The Torture Wrack stuck
a gothic tag on the grind of your self-inquisitorial doubt.

Such was the jargon of your late-teenage years;
how, back then, you talked to yourself.

Fragility

Cellophane is thin enough,
but too flexible.

Glass, while brittle,
is too resistant.

Tinsel is surprisingly
hard to snap.

Brick, mortar, steel—
those make you laugh.

Perhaps a soap bubble,
glistening, its fragility

its essence: yes,
that's you

when
bared

to
touch.

The Eruption

They creep in surreptitiously—
the little estrangements,

casual alienations,
disregarded disconnections

(they're so much just
part of the daily noise)—

then sink
to the bottom of your soul

where they rub up
against each other,

swell into dreams
then full-blown nightmares

until one day
you're just walking along

when a crack,
then an eruption,

splits
you apart.

Looking Elsewhere

Slipping into trouble,
emotionally,

is like watching,
mesmerized,

as your knees rise
like newly formed mountains

from the bathwater
while your back slides down

until, surprisingly—
even comically,

were anyone watching—
your head slips under.

The Filament

You hang on
to a filament

of faith
that sags

with the weight of the days
but doesn't snap,

only lowers you,
almost imperceptibly.

The Heavy Fall

You pace the room, then rooms, struck
aimless by the persistence of certain

uncertain memories, snow starting to
tumble around three, at first spare and

aimless, too, then with a heavier fall,
collecting and collecting until with

darkness its weight—the storm
turns out to be locally historic—

can be heard across the valley
buckling roofs.

The Lever

You find comfort in darkness,
dampness, retreat.

In seeing sidewalks
you don't care

to stride
glisten with rain.

In hearing cars
you don't care

to ride
hiss in the street.

You find comfort in darkness,
dampness, retreat.

Which asks only
that you depress,

deep within,
the lever of release.

The Autopsy

You perform the autopsy
yourself.

Put your lungs and intestines
in a cold steel pan.

Seal your heart
in a lidded jar.

That everything
keeps functioning

independently
amazes you.

Or, at any rate, amazes
the severed brain

conducting
the dismembering.

Division

So terrible is your dream
a strange face

turns within it
to attack the dreamer.

No more can you sleep
without his protection.

Those hurt, blazing eyes
defending you

against yourself—
whose are they?

Those stranger's eyes crying,
What have you done to him?

Your Prosecutor

Only half-awake, lingering
in dreams, you see him,

your prosecutor,
not as he appears

in the dock—
fine-tailored, worldly, shrewd,

his comprehensive knowledge
of your conflicted mind

flawlessly documenting
your career in self-crime;

no, he appears—
and you know it's him—

as if stripped
of that mask, revealing—

like a pen-and-ink illustration
from some Charles Dickens novel—

a gnarled, nasty, shrunken, smelly,
bile-filled, treacherous, fabricating,

evil
old man.

In joy, you draw awake,
rising up to kill him.

But the inky image
awakes along with you

and, laughing in mockery,
morphs—

as if computer-generated,
a nifty special effect—

back into your knowing,
relentless prosecutor,

a trickster, only fooling
with you.

Mantras

You wake up anxious
and, lying in bed, say

to yourself,
I was lost but now I'm found.

It's okay to be; it's okay to be me.
This is just pain from an old war wound.

But nothing unclamps
the vise on your chest

so you say,
Life got me into this; life will get me out.

This is just a stress fracture.
Just more comedy.

But no go and you need
to make it through this day

so you say,
Groundless fears cannot stand long.

I am stronger than self-defeating lies.
This is just the bridge toll to a new life.

Which clicks, your chest drains
away and you get up on legs

trembling from the weight of knowing
they must take you to brush your teeth

so, stumbling along, you say,
These are just the pains of rebirth.

Live it down by living it up.
You've fought with your devils, now dance with your angels.

And in this way
you get through this day.

A Moment in The Sun

As you sit outdoors at a small café,
sun easing your cares,

all the pigeons in the square
abruptly fly away

and you feel a sudden lightness
you haven't felt in years.

As if the pigeons were griefs
you'd kept longer than memory,

longer than mourning,
longer than reason or heart should allow.

Shaken free, you bolt up
to start your new life

when all the pigeons, as if startled
by their strange, exalted flight,

fly back down,
blackening the sky.

Dream Triptych

I

An old wooden sleigh
trundles fast downhill,

a woman sitting behind you,
embracing you, her heart

pounding against your back,
both of you sweaty, animalistic, made

intimate by shared excitement
as you scoop a ravine and sweep

up its sharp rise, then, meeting
level ground,

slow by a farmhouse
with a rustic old barn, finally

stopping before
an ash pit filled

with burnt sticks
and the leg of a human corpse.

You turn and cry, in warning,
It's a killing ground!

But though you see
no soldiers

with pointed rifles,
the woman is gone.

II

You float
down a river on a raft,

alone.
Then the river ends,

the rest of it
under construction.

You notice that
the motley survivors

are those necessary for a funeral:
a carpenter, a gravedigger, a priest,

and you
to play the final, solemn drum roll.

III

You walk a dirt path
in a strange, spare land.

Clothes in tatters.
Sun healing your back.

I am poor,
you say to all who stare

as if at the passing dead,
Yet my walk is rich.

Still Here

It seems you're
over the crying part.

Over the involuntary
shaking.

The chest vise
and night sweats.

You won't say you're serene,
of course,

but you think you'll
get by.

It's like when you spin
out on the road, twirling away

from an oncoming car
and coming to rest

without even
clipping a tree.

In the next moment—
still, silent, pre-relief—

all you know is that, somehow,
you're still here.

Journey to Heaven

The rising soul, in old Hollywood movies,
sits up as if summoned by death

and walks out of frame,
leaving behind its still-warm body.

Your home movie deliverance
unspools in reverse:

after abandoning
your soft, susceptible body,

your hardened soul returns
as if summoned by life.

It enters your old room
from out of frame,

walks up to your still, warm body
and, home again, lies down.

The Denial

The fever of dread
broken,

the cool of calm
issuing in,

(to get this far took you
nine countless years)

you find normalcy
disorienting,

even, somehow,
unreal,

the bond to your old warden
truer

than your bond with anyone
here on the outside.

Yet you must find
the strength

to deny him and—
betraying

your long, scrupulous intimacy—
declare: *Let him be strange.*

Traveling in India

The train is so crowded
you hang out the rear door,

lurching from stop to stop.
Commuters struggle to get on and off.

But you're there for the distance,
trying to write your impressions

while clinging to the back
though, in fact, your fellow travelers

are forcing you out of
the private compartment you bought.

They'd entered with such an air
of authority and entitlement you figured

this must be how it's done here, and,
considering how jammed the train was,

it seemed churlish, unkind,
not to give way.

But still you feel, as the hours wear on,
an anger and resentment—no one even seems

aware that it is you
who has a right to this place—

so when a train conductor happens along—
a young woman in a crisp blue uniform—

you ask her if this is right,
the done thing, okay.

Not at all, she says.
In fact, she says, it's quite odd:

this is yours, you paid for it,
you just need to tell everyone so.

And when you speak up, lo and behold the others
clear out without too much fuss and you write

in peace, the landscape—gorgeous, teeming,
variable, lost in time—serenely passing by.

At a scheduled layover, you ask
if you can leave your compartment

and if you do, will your work
still be there when you return.

The conductor laughs and says,
of course—just lock the door.

So you explore
the marvelous Indian city,

its wondrous bazaars and pungent foods;
even find a jeweled ring at a bargain price—

all you can afford—
to bring home to your patient wife.

Then another of the conductors, off duty,
invites you home where her husband

and a friend—both actors—perform—
as they say they would for any guest—

a highly stylized, heartbreaking
Indian play.

And when you return
to your compartment on the train

all is just
as you left it.

It ends lovely, this dream,
and means a lot to you.

Repairs

The flat, loosely fitted
fieldstones of the fence

that runs past here
change, in places,

to round stones
pointed with cement.

Repairs, perhaps.
Perhaps, while not as pretty, stronger there.

This old stone fence that,
curving as it recedes from you,

seems like looking
down the years.

watching ourselves
RECEIVE

Billie

The café was loud
and the sound system soft
so the music—Billie Holiday—
got lost unless you
listened for it, picked it out
from the table chatter and kitchen clatter
and from the flushed worker dropping
flatware fresh from the dishwasher
into a divided metal bin—from
the busy, vibrant, everyday
surface sounds that served
to camouflage Billie's
quiet voice; to shroud
her scarring devastation yet
helpless hope for love; to conceal
her gritty, intimate blues
so near to completely
that her rhythm section
was discernible not in itself
but only through what Billie
made of its measured flow of time
as she anticipated and lagged behind
then sank into the heart
of its passing.

After the Museum

After the museum, the canvas oil paintings, all
stiffly self-sufficient, march from my memory

while the watercolors—wispy, pastel swirls on
delicate paper—I close my eyes and remember;

watercolors of stray, fleeting, overlooked
moments that, together, capture and frame

a portrait of the body
of my days.

Drumming Essentials

The elegant avalanche
        of Elvin Jones; from Art Blakey,
                headlong, cliff-crashing waves.

The crackling, advancing brush fire
        of young Tony Williams matched
                by Max Roach, a mature forest maze.

With Roy Haynes
        ever bustling and weaving and
                brilliant as late-night, big-city streets.

Such were the essentials
        of some of the oversize gods
                who roamed the earth when I was a boy

with nothing more
        than a pair of drumsticks,
                a set of ears, and a need

to explore—
        guided by the ecstatic syntax
                of these gods' rhythmic codes—

my own
        essential
                unknowns.

The Caricature

Standing at a stupendous round table, twenty or so
corpulent, white-bearded men in black tuxedos

raise a toast to their shared and well-deserved
entitlements in this Arko Liqueurs advertisement

from pre-WWI Vienna, the poster a frothy
caricature that cuts, the illustrator puncturing

the gathering's bourgeois self-esteem while
slyly pedaling their privileges for a product;

the jolly men and keen satirist—if in opposite
ways—each sure they know—back on the eve

of the war to end all wars—
the way of the world.

watching ourselves
AGE

Aunt Alice

As my great-aunt Alice
advanced in age, she
lost her presence of mind.

Out, one day, for a leisurely drive,
we took her past the crumbling house
she'd spent most of her life

and Alice, seeing it,
excitedly cried, "Oh!
Let's go visit Alice!"

I quietly laughed,
my wife quietly cried,
then Alice quietly said,

as we passed the house by,
"I sure miss that old gal."

The Neighbor

It was sleep, not death.
We knew he'd wake up.

But at eighty-seven, our neighbor
seemed to be leaving us nap by nap,

each sunk into more easily
and harder to awaken from.

Today, losing his train
of thought, he fell asleep

even as he spoke. Though
his thought wasn't like a train, really.

More like a jumble of cars
heaped in the yard

of his long-term memory,
where his beginning and his end—

the prime of his journey already lost—
now rest.

Winter Sky

The cloud cover
holds, for the moment,

looming snow
as an old man, leaning on

his cane, approaches
from down a long country lane,

his dark coat
tight to his throat, its angled collar

raised to his wool cap,
his beard

the same
tarnished silver

as the threatening
clouds.

Then he stops and looks up
as if to take measure

of where he is
and how far he has to go

and how soon the sky
will unload

its cold weight, his
bearded face

blending into
the heavens

so vanishing,
his dark

winter clothes
an empty shell.

Bedtime

I see an elderly man
sitting alone on the edge of a bed
looking back to where his wife once slept.

Then I see him
taking off his eyeglasses
and setting them on a nightstand
then, with some effort, pulling off each shoe and sock
before standing and emptying his pockets of things—
keys, coins, wallet—
that join the eyeglasses.

Then I see him
frowning while fingering these nightstand objects
as if they were emblems of everyday abilities—
vision, access, profiting—become
stolen by age.

Then I see him
sitting and undressing
and leaving his clothes in a bedside heap
while, stripped, slipping in under the sheet
on his side of the bed.

Then after he fixes
his cloudy eyes
on the dimming, flickering
nightstand light, I see him,
with a soft, trembling hand,

reach out.

Bread

His fierce cancer
turned him fiercely suicidal
but too frail for it.

Then his further decline
drew the mind
that wanted to die
to revert
to reaching—hands trembling—
for bread
he'd slowly chew and savor.

Then he'd vanish
into his vacant stare,
his restless legs, his weak attempts
to pull his sheet and johnny coat off.

His beard gray and long
as an Old Testament prophet's,
it was life itself
with or without his approval,
testifying through him.

watching ourselves
VENTURE OUTDOORS

Snowflakes

stream
down the winter dark
with the ease
of passing hours, the stream
slowly thickening
to a blizzard of hours—
all the hours, it suddenly seems,
of all our lives
crystallized and coursing
by on this briefly
brilliant night.

Shadow Casting

Lit by a low
cloud cover,

each of its leaves
casting

soft darkness
on others,

the oak tree
stands

worshipfully
still

as if
praying

for an intricate,
long-held

grief
to lift.

The Summer Night

The calm summer night
out the open window seems

another room of the house,
an adjoining interior, a stroll

past the screen door offering
no transition, no contrast,

the deep night domesticated,
the full moon a reading lamp

left on to illuminate
the sacred, enigmatic

text
of home.

About the Poet

Mark Belair's poems have appeared in numerous journals, including Alabama Literary Review, Atlanta Review, The Cincinnati Review, Harvard Review, Michigan Quarterly Review, Poetry East and The South Carolina Review. His previous collections include Breathing Room (Aldrich Press, 2015); Night Watch (Finishing Line Press, 2013); While We're Waiting (Aldrich Press, 2013); and Walk With Me (Parallel Press of the University of Wisconsin at Madison, 2012). He has been nominated for a Pushcart Prize multiple times. Please visit www.markbelair.com

www.ingramcontent.com/pod-product-compliance
Lightning Source LLC
Chambersburg PA
CBHW031145090426
42738CB00008B/1231